WRITERS & READERS in association ... IN PAPERBACKS London · Sydney

This edition first published by Writers and Readers
Publishing Cooperative in association with
Unwin Paperbacks 1986

A *Writers and Readers* ➤ Documentary Comic Book © 1986

UNWIN ® PAPERBACKS
40 Museum Street, London WC1A 1LU, UK

Unwin Paperbacks
Park Lane, Hemel Hempstead, Herts HP2 4TE, UK

Writers and Readers Publishing Cooperative Society Limited
144 Camden High Street, London NW1 0NE, UK

Writers and Readers Publishing Inc.
500 Fifth Avenue, New York NY 10110

George Allen & Unwin Australia Pty Ltd
8 Napier Street, North Sydney, NSW 2060, Australia

Unwin Paperbacks with the Port Nicholson Press
PO Box 11–838, Wellington, New Zealand

Art Director: Janet Siefert

ISBN 0 04 927011 7

Beginners Documentary Comic Books are published by Writers and
Readers Publishing Cooperative Ltd, and Writers and Readers Publishing
Inc in association with Unwin Paperbacks. Its trademark consisting of the
words "For Beginners, Writers and Readers Documentary Comic Book"
and the portrayal of a seal bearing the words "Beginners Documentary
Comic Books" and Writers and Readers logo is registered in the U.S.
Patent and Trademark Office and in other countries.

Printed in Great Britain by Richard Clay (The Chaucer Press) Ltd, Bungay,
Suffolk

Elvis

FOR BEGINNERS

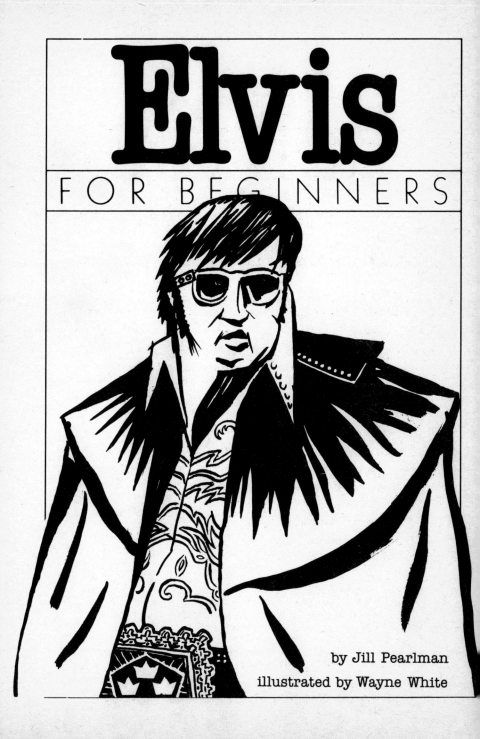

by Jill Pearlman

illustrated by Wayne White

History books tell you that America has no kings—no doubt the books written before 1956. Elvis is an American king—people's choice, feet of clay, king stud.

Our butch boy king ticked off a revolution—the takeover of high culture by popular culture. In this process of democratization, Elvis represented the whole underclass—young, poor, black—for whom opera and existentialism meant as much as "veni, vidi, vici." What mattered? Rawness, energy and instinct. And who eventually succumbed but America, who's always believed that truth lies in the untamed.

Boil Elvis down to the facts and he still evokes like an over-written American roots saga. It's a Southern saga, but at the core either black or white. Elvis rose from the desperate segment of Southern society shared by all poor people.

Consider two key terms in the standard biography:

The Legend of Elvis

"The son of sharecroppers, Elvis Presley was born in a shotgun shack in Tupelo, Mississippi on January 8, 1935."

Sharecroppers: Farmers who worked fields for white plantation owners and received a share of the crops' profits. A successor to the slavery system.

Shotgun Shack: A wood frame house hardly larger than an outhouse. Why was it called "shotgun"? According to some, because a bullet could enter the front door and exit the back without hitting a thing.

Gladys Smith Presley
(1912-1958)

Originally sharecroppers, the Smiths moved to East Tupelo, home of the newly industrialized garment industry. Gladys worked roughly 7 hours a week for $13 as a sewing machine operator when she married at age 21. Later worked as a seamstress and laundress. Shared an unusually intimate, intense relationship with Elvis, who called her "Satnin.'"

Vernon Presley
(1916-1979)

Worked as a sharecropper hoeing cotton, corn and peas when he married at age 17. In 1937, when Elvis was 2, was sentenced to three years at Parchman Penitentiary for forging a check by altering the figures. Most details have been squelched. Later, drove a milk truck, packed crates of paint cans and managed his son's personal business affairs.

Elvis may have been as common as a kid with a scratch, but his parents treated him like an heir apparent.

A neighbor reported, "Gladys thought he was the greatest thing that ever happened and she treated him that way. She worshipped that child from the day he was borned to the day she died."

Elvis corroborated, "My mama never let me out of her sight. I couldn't go down to the creek with the other kids. Sometimes when I was little, I used to run off. Mama would whip me, and I thought she didn't love me."

Under his parents, Elvis develops two lifelong habits. Extreme Deference. . .

. . . and Extreme Self-Indulgence. In spite of poverty, Elvis's every whim was catered to; being a good boy, he never argued.

Elvis Aron was born a twin to Jesse Garon, who unfortunately died at birth. But did he really die?

It's said that Elvis, at age five, began to hear Jesse Garon's voice and regularly spoke to his "psychic soulmate" throughout his adult life. Elvis's dead twin also comes to earth regularly in the tabloids.

Elvis Was a Weird Teenager Who Talked To His Dead Twin Brother

Startling new insights into the strange, tragic life of Elvis Presley are given by author Elaine Dundy in her fascinating new book, "Elvis and Gladys." In the following exclusive ENQUIRER installment from his dead book, Dundy reveals how as a teenager Elvis often talked with his dead twin brother — and how he lost one of the greatest loves of his life.

By ELAINE DUNDY

Elvis Presley was born a twin, possibly an identical twin, but his brother Jesse died at birth — and the fact that the very beginning of Elvis' life marked the end of his brother's affected him throughout his life.

He felt loss and guilt over having been the twin to live. But he also felt triumphant. He was, after all, the one who had survived. Did this not prove that he was the strongest? ... himself narrowly escaped death when, at the age of 1, a ...

Next Week: Elvis Sells His Soul To the Man Who Made Him a Superstar

He Found His Idols

...ARVEL JR. inspired Elvis' glisten... ...ed onstage. Elvis loved... ...in high

"They say when one twin dies, the other grows up with all the qualities of the other too . . . If I did, I'm lucky."

Take Jesse as a "psychic soulmate" and we have a handle on the impossible—explaining Elvis's dual nature. Everyone has contradictions, but the king is Janus incarnate. He was both quintessentially hip and quintessentially square, iconoclastic and unifying, as sublime as any mortal can be and utterly, slavishly mundane.

To one Elvis biographer, Albert Goldman, these contradictions suggest that our hero was mad, an outright schizophrenic. But contradictions yielded him success—like the world's largest variety store, he had something to offer everyone. And accordingly, everyone took something completely different. Elvis was reinvented millions of times over, leaving the infamous Sybil, who had 17 personalities, in the dust.

Into what kind of world
was Elvis born?

One suffering from . . .

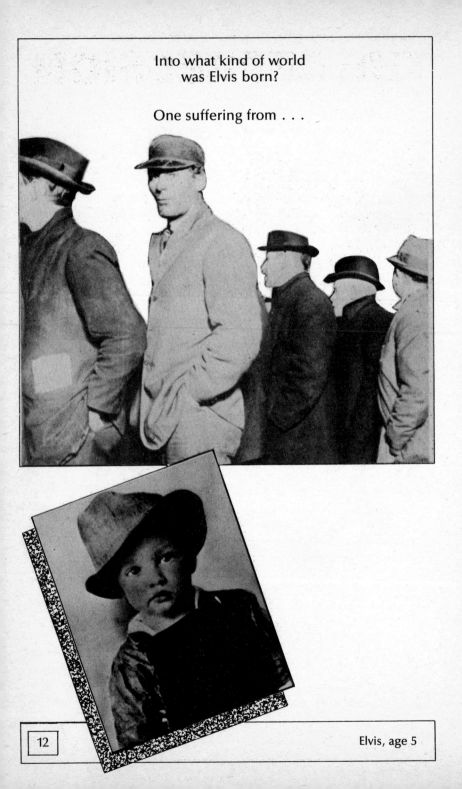

Elvis, age 5

THE DEPRESSION

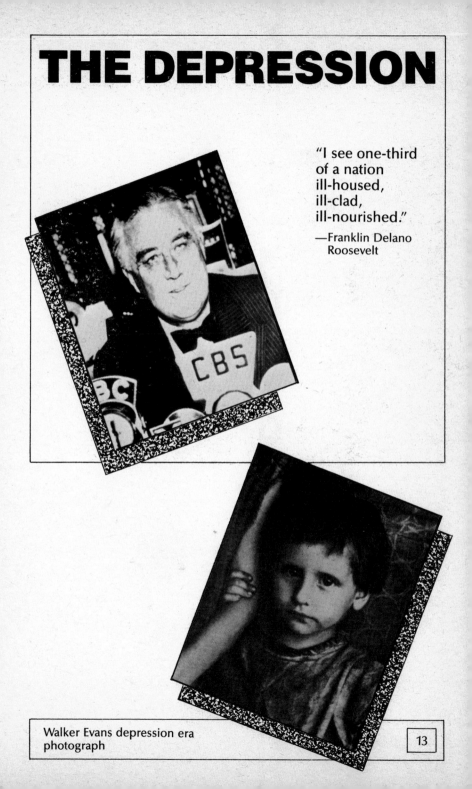

"I see one-third
of a nation
ill-housed,
ill-clad,
ill-nourished."
—Franklin Delano
Roosevelt

Walker Evans depression era
photograph

The newly elected President Roosevelt tried to stir a country close to rigor mortis since the stock market crash of 1929. Never had the mechanics and the morale of the country been so stilled, or suffering so well understood.

"Let me assert my firm belief that the only thing we have to fear is fear itself . . . This nation asks for action, and action now. We must act, and act quickly."

1933: Sixteen million—one in three workers—are unemployed. Over one dozen banks declared "Bank holidays."

Within 100 days, a special section of Congress swept through 15 new laws, the thrust of the New Deal: TVA, NRA, PWA, AAA.

Just 33 days before FDR's 1933 inauguration, Adolf Hitler is elected Germany's new chancellor.

1939: Hitler invades Poland, touching off World War II.

FDR allows Britain and France to purchase ammunition on a "cash-and carry basis."

December 7, 1941—Japanese bomb Pearl Harbor.

December 8—Congress declares war on Japan.

December 11—Germany and Italy declare war on the U.S.; Congress reciprocates.

$ FDR: $

The Nation's

ECONOMIC PROBLEM #1

The Depression hit the South like a bag of bricks. Per capita income was $797 around the country, except in the South where it scraped to $372. In 1931, cotton cost a nickel a pound, the worst price of the century. New clothes were on few people's shopping list.

Stripped of its prosperous patina, the "New South" became the same old hokey South in Northern eyes. It was, to Yankees, a tangled, hot, emotional mesh, not quite a jungle but a place where rationality had little sway, where passions and freak streaks of madness, gaudiness, violence and plain weirdness erupted.

The flourishing Fundamentalist religions were considered extreme and bizarre in their fanatic skew to the soul (not the intellect) and to uncontrolled emotional outpourings. To fundamentalists, black and white, speaking in tongues, writhing, singing, and other paroxysms were signs of God-given salvation.

Little did detractors know that rock 'n roll was being nurtured in church. And from church some of the country's best musicians would spring, able to exploit common property—soul, spirit, inspiration, fervor, emotionalism. The blues may deal with sex in the present; gospel with redemption in the future. But they're both about transmuting the ordinary, about the soul's turmoil and its search for satisfaction.

"The blues are a lot like church. When a preacher's up there preaching the Bible, he's honest to God trying to get you to understand things. Well, singing the blues is the same thing."

—Lighting Hopkins

GOSPEL JUBILEE

FRI. SEPT. 17 1953

So volatile was emotion, Pentecostals insisted, that it must be restricted to church and gospel; all other emotional expression belonged to the Devil. Elvis questions easy divisions.

In African religions, there was no Satan. Music was so integral to life it sometimes went unnamed. Yes, when converted, the American slaves took passionately to Christianity. But they integrated into it their own spirit, and the church became a bedrock of African tradition. For instance, the old dictum, "The spirit will not descend without a song" became gospel in their churches.

The Presleys belonged to the First Assembly of God, the largest white Pentecostal sect. Elvis notes the deft artistry of preachers who cut and paste their own interpretations of the Bible—the more original, the more authentic their choice by God. Elvis will do the same. Everything J.S. Bach did was for the glory of God; same with Elvis. But in his theology, the new god is a broad-minded deity of all life—love, sex, nature, as in African theologies. While Elvis's across-the-board gospel fervor makes perfect sense to him, others will question:

"Isn't that pelvis shake a little odd for church?"

His is like any non-Christian religion that celebrates puberty or fertility rites. Rock itself became a modern romantic cult with rites of purification and affirmation.

Estranged from most white churches of restraint, the white Pentecostals were really cousins of the traditional black churches of emotion. In church, whites could get "release"—they could be spontaneous, spiritual, sensual, i.e. they could be "black." That's not all they shared—like slipping mountain climbers on a rope, they clung to the Bible's "Last shall finish first" prophecy. They placed their faith in the afterworld, the otherworldly and the supernatural, vehemently repelling modern science and a world which had rejected them.

Okay, in the hot backwaters of cultural isolation and defensiveness, rock 'n roll was beginning to boil. Let's talk music.

NEW RELEASE No. 9
GET ON BOARD
LITTLE CHILLUN'
No. 133

FREDDIE SLACK Orchestra with the Mellowaires
Vocal—ELLA MAE MORSE
From Hollywood

A Capitol Records release, 1943

THE ROOTS OF
ROCK 'N ROLL

"All we did
was take
country music
and give it
a colored beat."

—Carl Perkins

Lightnin' Hopkins

While the forms of African music changed when brought to America (for starters, drum playing was outlawed), principles have to this day remained the same— immediacy, complex rhythmic drive, rapt vocals, raw emotion. Slaves sang field hollers, spirituals and sorrow songs, from which evolved the blues. The blues don't wallow; they're as much about suffering as the beauty of the backbone; they stomp the blues with the joy of being alive—if for no other reason than to play music.

White settlers sang long, narrative ballads brought from the British Isles. Largely arhythmic and sung in a thin, nasal whine, they recount narratives of mournful, tragic, violent and weird tales, mainly about those who transgress the community's covenants. Their beauty lay in their compelling eerieness and sense of unavoidable tragedy. At the heart is tension—breaking loose is always at one's fingertips, but the price is having one's hand cut off.

**Whites
gave blacks
the guitar**

In spite of the purported segregation, a good deal of exchange took place. For the slaves, acculturation began almost immediately; the result was their music became not African, but American. For instance, many plantation house slaves learned to play European harmony on European instruments (violin, fife and flute), and formed slave orchestras. They picked up brass instruments and, with a nod to Napoleonic France, formed the very common marching band.

If country rebels assumed the blacks' obsession with freedom and distaste for guilt, the rest picked up on their hot rhythms. True to the stereotypes, many white kids learned the blues on an old slave's knee, and many blacks made good by entertaining whites. Travellers and members of medicine shows became the links between the musics of rural blacks and whites. A whole pool of tunes became common to both races.

Blacks
gave whites
the banjo

In 1845, an anonymous writer in Knickerbocker Magazine wrote, "Who are our true rulers? The Negro poets, to be sure. Do they not set the fashion, and give laws to the public taste? Let one of them, in the swamps of Carolina, compose a new song, and it no sooner reaches the ear of a white amateur, than it is written down, amended (that is, almost spoilt), printed, and then put upon a course of rapid dissemination, to cease only with the utmost sounds of Anglo-Saxondom, perhaps with the world. Meanwhile, the poor author digs away with his hoe, utterly ignorant of this greatness."

AM I NOT A MAN AND A BROTHER?

Every culture evolves through innovation, imitation and transformation. But more often than not in American music, blacks provided the genius and whites the popular interpretation. Beyond that, blacks received only just a nod of appreciation, sometimes posthumous fame, while white musicians enjoyed the spoils. (In response to appropriation, black music was constantly innovating; in contrast, country music steadfastly remained the same.)

With its crooked, perverse ironies, the history of minstrelry would fit like hand into glove into the theater of the absurd. Around 1840, 20 years before the Civil War, blacks were personae non gratae. White entertainers, however, were smearing their faces with burnt cork to look black — comic revues of the ragtime songs, jokes and habits of blacks were hot. To get work, you had to look black; if you were black, you couldn't get work.

After the Civil War, instead of doing minstrels in their own style, blacks began imitating whites imitating blacks. And with a dose of real black humor, they smeared their faces with cork.

There's no copyright on culture.
It's said that Ma Rainey, Mother of the Blues, came upon her form this way:

"I was singing minstrel and popular songs with a black tent show, the Rabbit Foot Minstrels. In about 1902, when we were going through a small Missouri town, I heard a girl singing about a man who left her in a strange and poignant way. None of us had heard anything like that before. I worked it into my act, and the response I got? Everywhere I went, I looked for those songs, and added them to my repertoire."

Ma

28

RISE OF THE RECORD INDUSTRY

"When you get in the record business, someone gonna rip you anyway so that don't bother me. If you don't rip me, she gonna rip me, and if she don't rip me, he gonna rip me, so I'm gonna get ripped . . . "
—Muddy Waters

COLUMBIA DOUBLE-DISC RECORDS
MUSIC ON BOTH SIDES

Columbia advertisement, c. 1905

T he recording industry lived on Tin Pan Alley songs, cheery, mindless show tunes or show tune imitations. In the 20s, when portable recording techniques were developed, recording began "on location" in the rural South. The markets were divided into "hillbilly" and "race" music.

B ack to Elvis, who, while we were digressing won second prize at the Mississippi-Alabama Fair and Dairy show for singing "Old Shep." Shortly thereafter, Elvis asked his parents for a bicycle. But mother knows best: Gladys bought him a $12.95 guitar instead.

Cousin Hershell Presley: "I remember Elvis used to carry that ol gi-tar around. He loved that gi-tar. It didn't have but three strings on it most of the time, but he sure could beat the dickens outta it."

CLUB

In 1948, the Presleys make an all-out effort to ditch poverty, pack up their belongings and move to Memphis. Not only was the city a mecca for musicians (Delta blues, classic blues, white gospel, country), it was one of the great preserves of prostitution and violence. Imagine the gaudy tableau it offered a pubescent mama's boy.

VERNON:

Who gave a fig about originality? We were just trying to survive.

We became part of the mass movement to urban centers. In 1900, 15% of all Southerners lived in cities. By 1960, the figure had risen to 55%. For blacks, the exodus to the North began after World War I. Between 1940-1950, 1¼ million blacks left the South.

We became slum renters. Unpacking our '39 Plymouth, we moved into 572 Poplar Avenue, a dilapidated house you wouldn't wish on your mother-in-law. We had one room, no kitchen and a bathroom we shared with three other families. Good Lord Almighty, don't fool yourself into thinking it was clean.

I became a manual worker. For the next five years, I packed cans of paint into boxes. What was a good week? $38.50.

We became residents of a housing project. In 1949, we moved into the Lauderdale Courts, one-half mile from Beale Street. Elvis starts school at Humes High, still walked by his mother (that's my wife). The best thing about Lauderdale was its motto, "From slums to public housing to private ownership." Elvis showed them what to do with that.

Wars provoke change; for music and for society, World War II was revolutionary.

Before the piano, there could be no piano concertos; before amplification, there could be no rock 'n roll.

The electric guitar appeared in the late 30s. The first modern guitar hero, T-Bone Walker's mastery laid the rules of the game.

With electricity, Muddy Waters made the blues industrial, loud, searing and unnerving; a response in kind to urban Chicago life.

B.B. King's technique of holding, bending, quivering a note, then sliding to the next couldn't predate the technology.

As accompaniment to the blues, the electric guitar and tenor sax replace the acoustic guitar and harmonica.

Diffusion of a rigidly defined society had begun. As the conventional ruling class fades, gentility becomes history.

"Look at the American male of today. The cutaway coat is obsolescent, except for borrowed or rented wear at weddings . . . The tail coat is worn by only a very few of the well-heeled young . . . the dinner coat is worn less and less . . . the hard collar has likewise almost completely departed."

—Frederick Lewis Allen, journalist

The Breakers

Three Fifth Avenue mansions of the rich and powerful Vanderbilt family had been razed for office or apartment buildings; the Breakers, their Newport summer mansion, became a public museum.

Rosie the Riveter

The War gave both blacks and women chances to prove their mettle—blacks were fighting next to whites on the battlefields—the President's Committee on Equality of Treatment and Opportunity in the Armed Forces (Fahy Committee) ended racial segregation. Women filled a depleted work force at home; over six million women took jobs, and the number of working wives doubled. When inequities were keenly felt, consciousnesses were raised; group identities were kindled and liberation movements born.

Rejecting the old society's stodgy values, the new self-made ruling class valued the fast, the brash and the new. Being savvy, they began to admire and absorb the style of the ghetto.

"Goddammit, look! We live here and they live there. We black and they white. They got things and we ain't. They do things and we can't. It's just like living in jail."
—Richard Wright, *Native Son*

Picture Malcolm X, as he describes himself in his auto-biography. He wears a sharkskin zoot suit which balloons at the knees but is so narrow at the ankles that he has to remove his shoes before taking them off. He wears a big long coat, dark orange shoes and a new conk when checking out Lionel Hampton's big blues band at Boston's Roseland Ballroom in 1940.

"*Showtime*! People would start hollering about the last hour of the dance. Then a couple of dozen really wild couples would stay on the floor, the girls chang-ing to low white sneakers. The band now would really be blast-ing, and all the other dancers would form a clapping, shouting circle to watch that wild compe-tition as it began, covering only a quarter or so of the ballroom floor. The band, the spectators and the dancers, would be mak-ing the Roseland Ballroom feel like a big rocking ship. The spot-light would be turning , pink, yellow, green and blue, picking up the couples lindy-hopping as if they had gone mad. '*Wail, man, wail!*' people would be shouting at the band; and it *would* be wailing, until first one and then another couple just ran out of strength and stumbled off toward the crowd, exhausted and soaked with sweat."

Predecessors of rhythm and blues, jump blues made the blues jump. Everybody loved my jaunty, jivey Tympany Five. We cooked up boogie and shuffle with rhythm sections tougher than my wife—and they could swing, too.

LOUIS JORDAN

Later, jump combos like Amos Milburn's and Roy Milton's got less jazzy, rougher and made repetition into an art. Milton's "R.M. Blues" has saxes laying one riff—five notes—over and over again until you're dreaming that thing! Saxes said the whole new thing. They riffed and riffed—I mean hard stuff—until all hell broke loose.

Leroi Jones: "The purpose was to spend oneself with as much energy as possible and make the instruments sound as unmusical and unwestern as possible."

R & B was about attitude, as much as anything. It spoke a total lack of innocence, and a total celebration of it. Sowing wild oats was not just a phase anyone was going through. The connotations of its main word, beat—steady rhythm, sex, violence—neatly connote R & B.

WYNONIE HARRIS

BIG MAYBELLE

Big Joe Turner, Wynonie Harris and Big Maybelle shouted with as little subtlety as possible. Little Esther had her first hit at 14, but sounded, like all R & B singers, like she been around life a few dozen times.

BIG JOE TURNER

HANK WILLIAMS

Country probably absorbed more black elements in the 40s than in any other era.

Like Elvis, Hank Williams was less a person than a state of mind. His revolution effected by force of personality: his fusion of country with black blues and fast rhythms served up his ragged, whisky-soaked sense of alienation and urban dislocation.

Starting with Bob Wills and his Texas Playboys, country musicians responded to the national fad for boogie-woogie. They fused hot rhythms, speed and rollicking licks to their own sound.

Hillbilly boogie

or

Western swing

Introducing the unit of electric guitar, electric bass, steel and rhythm guitar, Ernest Tubb became "Father of Honky Tonk." His flat, folksy voice was nothing new; his high-spirit and rhythm was.

Honky-tonk

Wynonie Harris
RACE
"Around the Clock"

Joe Turner
RACE
"Shake, Rattle and Roll"

Louis Jordan
RACE
"Let the Good Times Roll"

Roy Brown
RACE
"Good Rockin' Tonight"

Fats Domino
RACE
"The Fat Man"

Willie Mae Thorton
RACE
"Hound Dog"

Dominoes
RACE
"Sixty-Minute Man"

Still *in vitro*, a 16-year-old is
culling ideas for the future—
about two years away. In his
hometown, the national
headquarters for white gospel,
Elvis discovers all-night sings.

Gospel is theater based on the
dynamic principles of the
flood—either that or the riptide.
If you don't lose yourself in the
swell of voice and emotion,
you've been to see junk. Decked
out in lurid iridescence, quartets
like Hovie Lister and the
Statesmen, and the Blackwood
Brothers unleashed their bag of
vocal tricks.

Come to Jesus
Come to Jesus
He will save
Come to Jesus
Just now, just now
Come to Jes-es-us
Just now
Co-o-o-ome
He will save you

Above, we have the traditional savior, Christ, communicating through His medium, gospel. But below, witness a hot new savior working through its own medium, rock 'n roll and radio.

"Then one morning she puts on a New York station
you know she don't believe what she heard at all
She started shaking to that fine, fine music
You know her life was saved by rock 'n roll."

Lou Reed

Watching the radio in Texas

RADIO

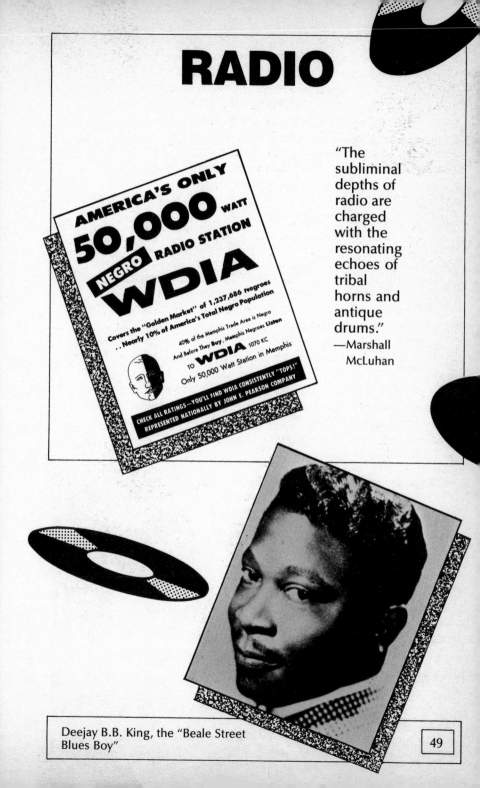

AMERICA'S ONLY **50,000** WATT **NEGRO** RADIO STATION **WDIA**

Covers the "Golden Market" of 1,237,686 negroes
.. Nearly 10% of America's Total Negro Population

40% of the Memphis Trade Area is Negro
And Before They **Buy**, Memphis Negroes **Listen**
TO **WDIA** 1070 KC
Only 50,000 Watt Station in Memphis

CHECK ALL RATINGS—YOU'LL FIND WDIA CONSISTENTLY "TOPS!"
REPRESENTED NATIONALLY BY JOHN E. PEARSON COMPANY

"The subliminal depths of radio are charged with the resonating echoes of tribal horns and antique drums."
—Marshall McLuhan

Deejay B.B. King, the "Beale Street Blues Boy"

49

Radio was an undeniable hero, the incredible traveling minstrel. WSM's Saturday night broadcasts of the Grand Ole Opry were a staple in every household, black, white or red. The only other Southern station to work such magic was the "Mother Station of the Negroes," WDIA. With a change in programming in 1948, it became the South's, and the country's, first black radio station. Now strangers by fate—Memphis opera divas, country fiddle pickers, barrel house pianists—could share the wealth of current black music.

WDIA was situated in Memphis; Memphis was thick with innovators and future stars gone on the manic frenzy of R & B. Across WDIA's wires came the whole scene, uncut and obscene—the bristling blues of local boys Sonny Boy Williamson and Howlin' Wolf, the newer sounds of Lloyd Price, Little Junior Parker, Ruth Brown and Bullmoose Jackson, whose "I Want a Bow-Legged Woman" couldn't wing it onto white radio. By 1954, WDIA had a core audience of over one million.

WMPS, one of Memphis's largest country stations, featured star DJ "Smilin'" Eddie Hill and local celebrity Bob Neal. Elvis used to watch Neal's live broadcast of High Noon Roundup, which featured country stars the first half hour and gospel groups the second. Later Neal tapped into some local talent—he became Elvis's manager.

Elvis and Gladys were radio junkies.

Up north in Cleveland, WJW Alan Freed discovered that teenagers were into black R & B. The record sales were right in front of him—he wasn't a visionary—but Freed was intrepid enough to act in the face of controversy. In 1952, he staged a rhythm review, tagged "Moondog's Coronation Ball." Swarms of black and white kids—three times the capacity of the Cleveland Arena—crashed it. He revamped his programming to bring the latest R & B to his gang of initiates. And he kicked off a nationwide craze.

Freed is said to have coined a new term for R & B—"rock 'n roll." Some significance lies in the transition. A powerful, explicit adult form was being altered for the innocence of the teen.

March, 1952: 21,000 kids crash Freed's Moondog's Coronation Ball.

51

Bill Haley (pictured here with Little Richard) looked less like a cool cat than an alley cat, but the guy did have some visionary blood. On the other hand, some cats you can't teach new tricks.

Columbia advertising Tony Bennett:

DIG THE CRAZIEST!!! HE SWINGS!!! HE ROCKS!!! HE GOES!!

RCA Victor advertising Perry Como:

DIG PERRY IN ACTION ON A GREAT ROCK-AND-ROLL RECORD

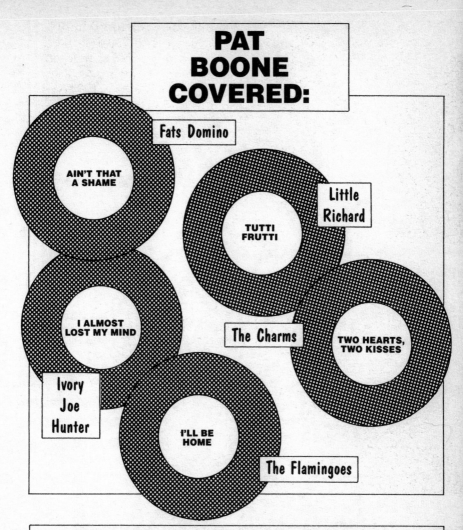

PAT BOONE COVERED:

Fats Domino

AIN'T THAT A SHAME

TUTTI FRUTTI

Little Richard

I ALMOST LOST MY MIND

The Charms

TWO HEARTS, TWO KISSES

Ivory Joe Hunter

I'LL BE HOME

The Flamingoes

Major label executives faced a dilemma: as civilized, cultured people, they were loathe to put out crap like rock 'n roll (nor were they as close to the bone as the indies), but who could pass up the bucks? Their solution: When a race (occasionally a hillbilly) hit began to break, they'd immediately assign a white artist to copy or "cover" it. This new version would be refined and emptied of its original meaning. Yet, as major radio stations refused to play songs with a black sound, the harmless white cover would become the money-making hit. If it sounds unfair, it was.

The flip side was that some listeners were lead back to the originals about which they'd never have known.

When he's not glued to the radio, Elvis is glued to the movie screen. He meets several men, mentors with a great deal to offer.

Hollywood held a cruel mirror. Bitterly, Elvis realized his life was as bland as a pan of cornpone.

Intuitively, he cast himself as a neo-Valentino, a Lothario, a Caravaggio. He's hot, but then again, cool as a magnet. Image preceded crystallization of ambition. He was a dreamy, determined narcissist.

His hair became a freestanding, independent deposit of vanity which had to be stroked at all times.

Red West, a friend from Humes High: "Elvis had his hair real long in those days. The rest of us had crew cuts. I remember once all the guys were gonna get him and cut his hair. I helped him escape from that." Elvis later rewarded Red by making him a core member of his entourage, the Memphis Mafia.

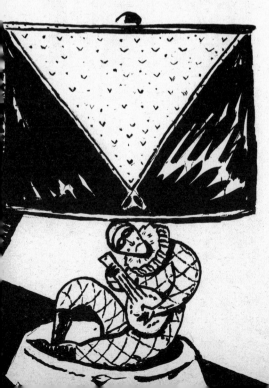

After graduating from Humes in 1953, Elvis worked for Precision Tool Company, then drove a truck for Crown Electric, an electrical contracting firm owned by James and Gladys Tipler. Although appalled that he frequented a beautician, Mrs. Tipler considered Elvis neat and polite.

High school graduation photo

SUN AND
THE KID WITH
THE SIDEBURNS

"If I could find a white boy who could sing like a nigger, I could make a million dollars."
—Sam Phillips

Of precarious twists and unlikely turns, the story of Elvis and Sun Records is perfect raw material for the folk tale it's become.

Marion Tipler

On a fall day, the kid with the pimples—I mean, sideburns—stopped into Memphis Recording Studio. A sideline of Sun, anyone could record two sides for $4.

He recorded two ballads. God knows, he wasn't Dean Martin. He had an earthiness, so I made a second recording for my boss, Sam Phillips, to hear.

Sam, he ignored it. When Elvis recorded two more tunes in January, '54, I again urged Sam to try the kid. Finally, Sam called Elvis. The kid ran so fast he nearly got arrested for speeding. When he sang, Sam was cool. But he teamed him up with guitarist Scotty Moore and bassist Bill Black to try and work something out. They rehearsed nearly every day after work to develop a style. Sam was waiting; he just said, "Keep it simple."

Phillips is one of rock's few untarnished legends. Just as rockabilly stands in a time warp as a pure classic, so does its creator, Phillips.

Gladys aside, Phillips was the first prescient genius to shape Elvis. He'd founded his studio in 1950 to tap top local talent (B.B. King, Junior Parker, Jackie Brentson, Howlin' Wolf), who otherwise had to record in Chicago. He liked music that communicated by way of the gut. What he envisioned was a new gut music to wow both white and black kids. He needed someone to embody it—someone white.

Sam's genius came in recognizing the wheat from the chaff, and it was the chaff—the rough stuff—that he wanted. Elvis's first record, "That's All Right, Mama," sprang from raucous clowning around after months of experimenting.

As early as his first record, Elvis didn't sound black—he went for too much finesse—but at the core of inspiration, he was a killer. What Elvis adopted was the black ego. What he avenged was alienation—being "white trash," a loner, a loser. What he crystallized was the sex-charged adolescent.

Phillips has said that if the feel wasn't there, if he couldn't get it in one take, he dropped the whole session. His blues approach to recording—each man totally unique, each man testing himself—was crucial to his conceptualizing of white rock 'n roll. He also utilized technology, the heavy echo, in a way that sharpened and deepened the record. With the echo, Elvis's voice quavers, lingers milliseconds, with otherworldly dimensions. In this 3-D atmosphere, Elvis has PRESENCE.

In September, 1954, Sun released
"Good Rockin' Tonight,"
otherwise known as

There's-ah good-ah rockin' to-naiiiiiight

The R & B tune was released twice before, in 1947 by its writer Roy Brown and one year later by blues shouter Wynonie Harris. Brown was a sophisticated blues crier known for the emotional intensity he poured into a song. Harris was more raucous, bawdy; he had a shaking pelvis not unlike Elvis's.

Unlike the earlier versions, Elvis's cuts clear from jazz. His displays a fresh, tight conception, another example of his unpredictable, imaginative Sun musical fusions. The trio becomes the rockabilly trinity. The three play so close they're practically in each other's minds.

Scotty Moore's clear, coherent guitar playing sets the style for rock 'n roll guitarists down the line. He develops both fast country runs and blues lines. High, ringing, heavily miked, he expounds upon Elvis's two sides—innocence and fury.

Bill Black's bass doesn't walk, it runs. He snaps his stand-up bass (slapback bass) with the palm of his hand, the mike fattening it with reverberations. The compulsive rhythm—with its accent on the second and fourth beats (backbeat)—is so strong drums would sink it.

By this time, Elvis was soaring as a local sensation. When DJ Dewey Phillips played "That's All Right, Mama," on his radio show, Red, Hot 'n Blues, the audience flipped. Its "ta dee dah dee dee dah" refrain became famous as a code phrase—hip kids used it as a greeting. And Elvis, Scotty and Bill began socking every small town in the deep South, playing almost 200 dates in one year.

ELVIS, SCOTTY and BILL

IN PERSON
★ Elvis ★
PRESLEY
SCOTTY and BILL
The "Blue Moon" Boys
For Dates—Write—Wire—Call
BOB NEAL
Exclusive Personal Management
160 Union Ave. Memphis, Tenn.
Phone: Office 8-2467; Home 4-4029

"This cat came out in red pants and a green coat and a pink shirt and socks, and he had this sneer on his face and he stood behind the mike for five minutes, I'll bet, before he made a move. Then he hit his guitar a lick, and he broke two strings. So there he was, these two strings dangling, and he hadn't done anything yet, and these high school girls were screaming and fainting and running up to the stage, and then he started to move his hips real slow like he had a thing for his guitar."—Bob Luman, young country singer who gave up trying to sound like Lefty Frizell and Webb Pierce

"The only band in history that was directed by an ass."
—Scotty Moore

If anyone knew how to advertise, it was Elvis. Between the still image and the demonstration, his pitch was impeccable, his offer irresistible—everyone had to have him. (There lay the tease—they couldn't. They could substitute with a record, a picture, a piece of his shirt, if lucky).

Elvis always put his strongest selling point—his pelvis—first. He cooly offered other attractions—loose guitar, slack mouth, brash stare. Each embodied a challenge; that challenge demanded a response. As Elvis banged out the beat, each person had the identical response in mind.

THE FIRST RIOT

It happened like a squirt of gasoline at a campfire. In closing his May 13, 1955 show, Elvis teasingly said, "Thank you. Girls, I'll see you backstage." That did it! Nearly half the audience, 7,000 driven, drunken girls, mobbed him. Those with safety pins scratched their names on his Cadillac; others smeared theirs on with lipstick.

While record companies noted the enthusiasm, they reacted cautiously. First off, the locale was the repressed Bible Belt where, naturally, an Elvis type would unleash sexual hysteria. Secondly, not only weren't Elvis's records charting nationally, they weren't even selling impressively locally. But in July, RCA-Victor had a sign—"Baby, Let's Play House" rose to number ten on the national country chart as Elvis's first charted single.

hmmmm...

Eagle-eye manager Colonel Tom Parker had also spotted Elvis. In this Southern cult, he saw more than money; he saw a hugely profitable national phenomenon. First, he won the Presley family's affections. Then he began negotiating a contract with major labels, ostensibly to help current manager Neal.

OFFICIAL
PRESS RELEASE:

Born West Virginia, 1910 to parents who traveled with a carnival.

Traveled with Great Parker Pony Circus from age ten.

At 17, had own pony and monkey act.

Became press agent in Tampa for carnivals and circuses.

Moved to Nashville where, in the 40s and 50s, managed top country singers Hank Snow, Gene Autry and Eddy Arnold.

November, 1955

RCA buys Elvis's contract from Sam Phillips for $35,000, and a $5,000 bonus for Elvis. The sum was extraordinarily high for a virtual unknown.

January, 1956

First of six TV appearances on Tommy and Jimmy Dorsey's Stage Show.

April, 1956

First RCA single, "Heartbreak Hotel," becomes number one on the Pop, Country and R & B charts after debuting on Stage Show. This three-market crossover sweep is unprecedented.

April, 1956

Just five months after singing with RCA, Hollywood movie producer Hal Wallis gives Elvis a screentest. He then signs him to a seven-year, three-picture, $450,000 deal. "I had the same thrill on seeing Errol Flynn for the first time," says Wallis.

"Okay, when does he go on?" —Ed Sullivan

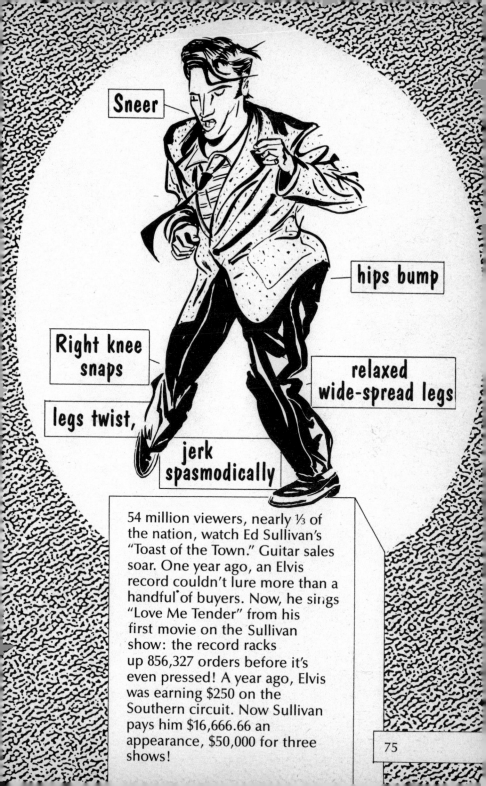

Sneer

hips bump

Right knee snaps

relaxed wide-spread legs

legs twist,

jerk spasmodically

54 million viewers, nearly ⅓ of the nation, watch Ed Sullivan's "Toast of the Town." Guitar sales soar. One year ago, an Elvis record couldn't lure more than a handful of buyers. Now, he sings "Love Me Tender" from his first movie on the Sullivan show: the record racks up 856,327 orders before it's even pressed! A year ago, Elvis was earning $250 on the Southern circuit. Now Sullivan pays him $16,666.66 an appearance, $50,000 for three shows!

The third show
shot Elvis
above the waist.
Why?

Harbinger of a new era

THE FIFTIES

"Hey mom, can I have a glass of milk and a hunk of cake?"
—Wally Cleaver

GOOD

Beauty Queens

Suburbia

TV

IKE... WE'RE BEHIND YOU 100%

Friedman's...first store in New England to sell out in order to buy complete new inventory

Ray Thorne Says Bango Is In National Spotlight

Credit

FRIEDMAN'S Executive Vice President Makes Statement

FRIEDMAN'S OPEN WEDNESDAY NIGHT
FROM 5 P.M. TO 11 P.M. TO START THIS GREAT

PROSPERITY SALE

MAKING $ MONEY

Hula Hoop

The 50s, the "Age of Normalcy," was like a TV dinner—bland, compartmentalized, worth about $1.89. It had no meat. It offered a few main courses (love of country, money, family), and was stingy when it came to sweets (cheerleading, necking). It required few decisions; one succumbed to its conformity. (TV dinners first appeared in the 50s, as did Muzak and Miltown.)

In 1952, former chief of staff of the Army, Dwight D. Eisenhower was elected President. He was pretty L7, you know, square. But even when fear of the Bomb hovered like a black cloud, Ike was anti-frantic, no sweat, negative perspiration.

By mid-decade, the cracks in the fragile construct were already apparent.

1954—Brown v. Board of Education of Topeka made separate black and white schools illegal. Integration was ordered "with all due haste."

Decline of the Cold War. Stalin died in 1953. Korean War ended 1954. Kinsey Report on Human Sexuality opened a new era of sexual discussion. McCarthy's reign of terror and purge of communists ended. He was censured by the Senate.

A new era was beginning in every facet of the arts:

Film: Godard, Truffaut, Fellini, Bergman

Literature: John Barth, Heller, Ferlinghetti

Art: Pollock, Newman, Rothko, de Kooning

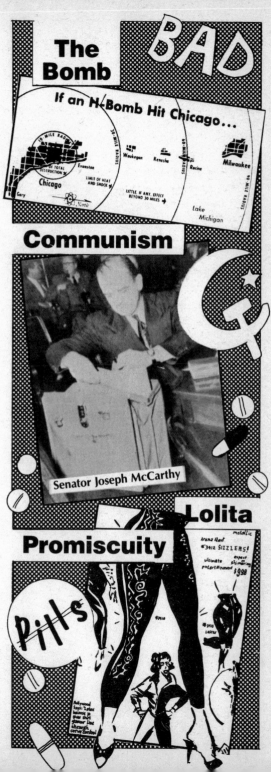

The Bomb

BAD

If an H-Bomb Hit Chicago...

Communism

Senator Joseph McCarthy

Promiscuity

Lolita

Pills

Enter the teenager, the most wrenching social invention since the *nouveau riche*. Suddenly, kids were the moneyed, leisure class. They reveled in it. They lived to consume and were consumed by it. Imagine Madame Bovary with a '56 Cad.

Newsweek photo, December 1958
Caption read: "For Want of Fresh air, hair turned green."

Society may squirm, it may squeal, but eventually it stoops to the conquerers. It strives to imitate—part of economic necessity, part of fashion. The entertainment industry was one of the first to go. For filmmakers, TV producers, record executives and radio DJs, success meant thinking like a 14-year-old.

The Incredible Shrinking Man
1957 science fiction film
What caused the shrinkage? Atomic mist

THE WHITE NEGRO

In his 1957 essay, Norman Mailer described a rebel who confronts the 50s "collective failure of nerve." He is the hipster—bohemian, juvenile delinquent and Negro fused. He gets his vital force from the Negro, with his "sophistication of the wise primitive in a giant jungle."

A new breed of adventurers, urban adventurers who drifted out at night looking for action with a black man's code to fit their facts." Mailer defined the hipster as a middle class American existentialist. But he didn't have to be so intellectual. Teenagers were naturals. In fact, Mailer compares the hipster's language to "a language most adolescents can understand instinctively, for the hipster's intense view of existence matches their experience and their desire to rebel."

JEAN·PAUL
SARTRE

Elvis was the White Negro of the teen masses. Naturally, parents didn't approve. It was as if they took literally Mailer's most creative phrases—"the decision to encourage the psychopath in oneself" or "the search for an orgasm more apocalyptic than the one which preceded it."

Couldn't they have branded Elvis a fringe lunatic? He was hardly fringe. His threat came in his unwieldy popularity. Elvis had clout.

So Elvis became the whipping boy of a nervous society. They called him a drug addict, a homosexual and a murderer. They accused him of causing juvenile delinquency, amorality and, at the very least, adolescent insolence. Elvis didn't flinch. At one point he said, "I don't mind being controversial. Even Jesus wasn't loved in his day."

WHY THEY ROCK 'N ROLL —AND SHOULD THEY?

HE CAN'T BE

In San Antonio, the city council banished rock 'n roll from city swimming pools and juke boxes because its primitive beat "attracted undesirable elements given to practicing their spastic gyrations in abbreviated bathing suits."

In Asbury Park, NJ, newspapers reported that 25 "vibrating teenagers" had been hospitalized after a record hop. The mayor prohibited all future rock concerts in city dance halls.

THE GREAT ROCK 'N ROLL CONTROVERSY

—BUT HE IS

Like most important art, rock offended the status quo. So bad was that 50s status quo that rock totally inverted its values ("he's not dirty bad, he's dirty good"). Rock was like the Statue of Liberty asking to recycle an old society's trash. If it hadn't gotten a rise, its makers probably would have gone corporate in despair.

"Aside from the illiteracy of this vicious 'music,' it has proven itself definitely a menace to youthful morals, and an incitement of juvenile delinquency. There is no point in soft-pedaling these facts any longer. The daily papers provide sufficient proof of their existence."
—The Music Journal

Trashing the literary tradition: Rock musicians took keen delight in making no sense, in languishing in that inventive, preverbal stage of baby talk, jibberish and nonsense.

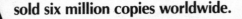

Trashing inhibition with exhibition: Elvis rolled the royal carpet for the intense, manic, hedonistic rockabilly dynasty—Carl Perkins, Roy Orbison, Charlie Rich, Johnny Cash and Jerry Lee Lewis.

"I think every one of them must have come in on the midnight train from nowhere. I mean, they came from outer space."
—Sun publicist Bill Williams

sold six million copies worldwide.

"Whole Lotta Shakin'"

"Great Balls of Fire"

Sun's best-selling record:

Trashing tasteful consumption and conservative dresswear: Elvis buys his mother a Crown Victoria Cadillac; naturally, it's pink.

"His world-construction is bound to be mainly a product of fantasy, and that his credulity is limited only by his capacity for conjuring up the unbelievable. And it is to say that he is a child man, that the primitive stuff of humanity lies very close to the surface in him, that he likes naively to play, to expand his ego, his senses, his emotions, that he will accept what pleases him and reject what does not, and that in general he will prefer the extravagant, the flashing, and the brightly colored."—W.J. Cash on the generic Southerner

"There was even a wild rumor that I shot my mother. Well, that's pretty silly. She's my best girl friend, and I bought her and Dad a home in Memphis where I hope they'll be for a long time. I made my father retire a few months ago. There isn't much sense in his working, because I can make more in a day than he can make in a year."
—Elvis

Elvis bought a $40,000 house on Audubon Drive in a genteel Memphis neighborhood. First neighbors complained about Gladys's rather ungenteel habit of hanging out the laundry. Then they brought a public nuisance suit over the constant flock of fans in front of Elvis's house. They considered Elvis, in the words of Newsweek magazine, "a jug of corn liquor at a champagne party." The judge reminded them that the Presley house was the only one paid in full; Elvis paid in cash while the others held mortgages or leases.

One year later, Elvis paid $100,000 cash for

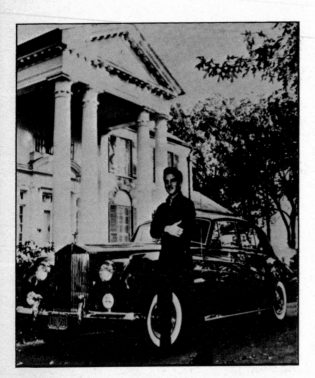

Where did police check first whenever a female runaway—from anywhere in the country—was reported? Naturally, in front of Graceland.

GRACELAND

"**I** don't know what it is. I just fell into it, really. My daddy and I were laughing about it the other day. He looked at me and said, 'What happened, El? The last thing I can remember is I was working in a can factory, and you were driving a truck.' We all feel the same way about it still. It just . . . caught us up."

"**T**he only chance for a humane society would be if Elvis Presley was President."
—Phil Ochs

In December 1956, Elvis appeared at a Christmas Goodwill benefit for Memphis radio station WDIA.

"**N**ever in your life have you seen such a surge of black faces converging on that stage. In a lifetime, I know of only one other person who could have that kind of magnetism. And that was Dr. Martin Luther King."
—DJ and musician Rufus Thomas

What if Elvis had become a truly biracial idol?

"Elvis opened the door so I could walk through. I thank God for Elvis Presley."
—Little Richard

"The colored folks have been singing it and playing it just the way I'm doing now, man, for more years than I know. Nobody paid it no mind till I goosed it up." —Elvis

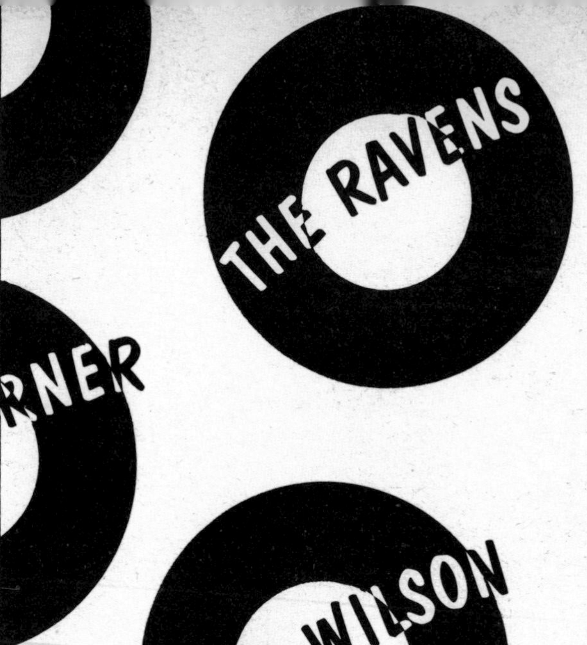

THE RAVENS

RNER

JACKIE WILSON

RAY CHARLES

JAMES BROWN

THE COASTERS

MORSE

DO...

LITTLE RICHARD

...S DOMINO

WYNON...

CHUCK BERRY

...COOKE

DOMIN...

THE ORIOLES

...E ROBINS

Rock 'n roll was a common ground for each race. By moving towards its middle point, blacks could and did gain unprecedented respect and access to white markets. Never before had there been so many black pop stars.

SOUL BROTHER #1

Elvis loved this country like I do. Loved cars. Loved his Daddy and Mama. Elvis was basic. And look how they done him.

Elvis had a great following among blacks, but you didn't see it. Blacks weren't allowed to be his followers. Do you think a black girl could run up and kiss him? The system wouldn't let us be together.

Elvis always had soul, or he couldn't have done those records.

BOTH ELVIS AND JAMES BROWN HAD:

☆ Groundbreaking hits in '56 (Brown's "Please, Please, Please")
☆ Extravagant sexual and emotional performing styles
☆ Dynamic religious-styled singing
☆ Pentecostal upbringings
☆ God-like status

From the start, Elvis was subdued and styled strictly for a white audience. Record company executives were interested in money, not integration. They hated rock and wanted houses in the suburbs to protect their kids from what it had wrought. As far as business went, the less black stain, the better.

Besides, Elvis himself was speeding on the mainstream. "Elvis was greatly anxious for success. He talked not in terms of being a moderate success. No—his ambition and desire was to be big in the movies and so forth. From the very first he had ambition to be nothing in the ordinary but to go all the way."
—Bob Neal

MISTER
WHITE BREAD?

Not enough groundwork had been laid for a 60s type of social revolution. The anti-rock reaction was rife with racism, and the most extreme examples occurred in its home, the South.

In April '56, the North Alabama White Citizen's Council accused the NAACP of using rock 'n roll in a plot to corrupt white Southern teenagers. They started a campaign to pressure radio to ban the "immoral" music.

Elvis Go GANG GO!!
PRESLEY SHIRTS
Only 1.99

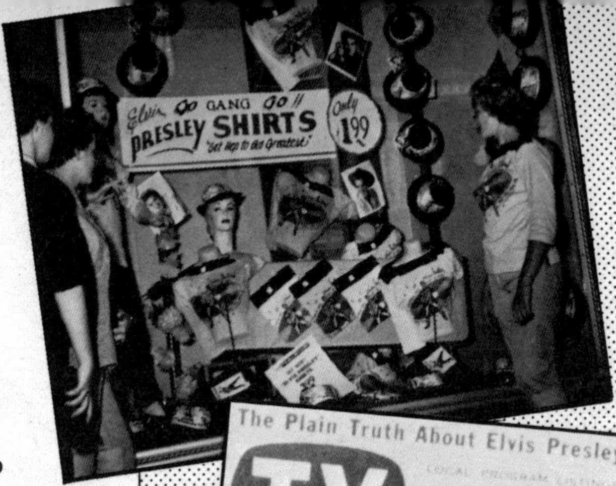

"When it's gone, I'll switch to something else. I like to sing ballads the way Eddie Fisher does and the way Perry Como does, but the way I'm singing now is what brings in the money. Would you change if you was me?"

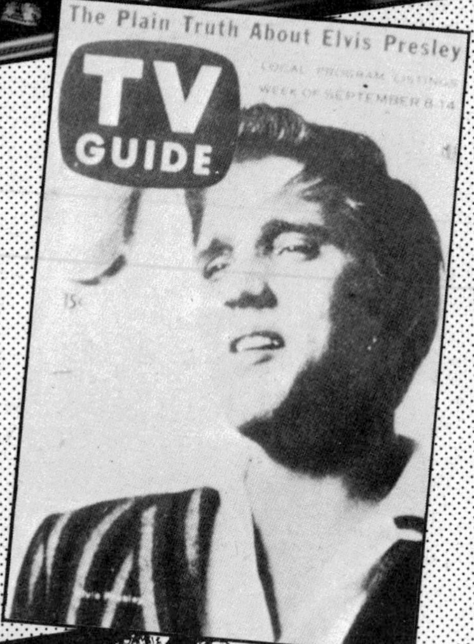

The Plain Truth About Elvis Presley
TV GUIDE
LOCAL PROGRAM LISTINGS
WEEK OF SEPTEMBER 8-14
15¢

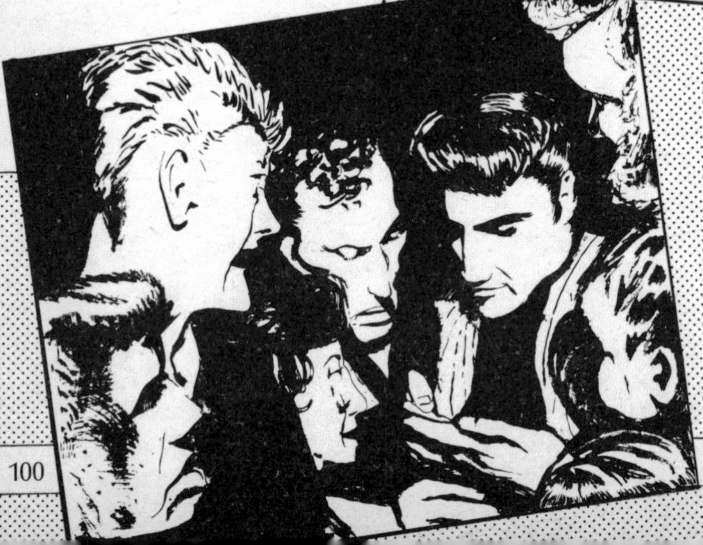

Chuck Berry, Little Richard, Jerry Lee Lewis, Buddy Holly and Carl Perkins all demonstrated musical commitment by creating original bodies of work. They wrote music and lyrics, and played instruments. Elvis didn't even prepare for sessions. He chose songs from a group selected by his publishing company and copied the demo, whose singer is trying to imitate him. But once down to singing, Elvis is meticulous, original, and virtually produces himself.

Now that Elvis belonged, the rebel stuff was over. He wants only to be liked more. By playing the histrionic, doomed Punk hero, he twists a constantly growing audience around his finger. His delivery is no longer desperate, but teasingly, playfully confident.

But Elvis's commerical streak was miniscule compared to Colonel Parker's. For Elvis's mass appeal, Parker wanted massive amounts of money and power. It was lust—and it was consummated. The brainchild was Elvis's career.

A ramblin' kind of guy

THE HOLLYWOOD HILLBILLY AND THE HOLLYWOOD HUSTLER

"I'd rather close a deal with the Devil."
—attributed to producer Hal Wallis

Starring in "Speedway"

Advertising "Dancing Chickens," Parker once hid an electric hot plate under straw and played the song, "Turkey in the Straw" while the poor animals hopped around.

THE COLONEL SAYS "HAVE A NICE DAY"

He sold foot-long buns with the ends of hot dogs sticking out. The Colonel's specialty was publicity. His strategy was to saturate the market on every level—grass roots, record stores, concert promoters.

ELVIS MONTHS—APRIL AND MAY

ELVIS KISSIN' COUSINS

on RCA VICTOR

In his later days, Parker hired all the midgets in Hollywood, most of whom had appeared in **The Wizard of Oz** to parade as the Elvis Presley Midget Fan Club.

By 1956, there were 78 different Elvis products and millions of dollars coming in every month. The Colonel gave Special Products, Inc., a Beverly Hills marketing firm, the licensing. He and Elvis collected a royalty of four to eleven per cent on the manufacturer's wholesale price. By the end of '57, Special Products president Hank Saperstein guessed he'd grossed $55 million.

THE COLONEL'S PIECE OF THE PIE

The Colonel's level of detail was pennies—he negotiated for every single one. He got 25% of all of Elvis's earnings in their first contract, a hefty cut. When they renegotiated in 1967, Parker managed to get a 50/50 split.

Songwriters who worked for Elvis had to agree to an unusual arrangement. Although he never wrote one song, Elvis's name was added as a co-writer; his publishing company received one-third of the royalties. (Elvis could easily make their songs hits. One-third of the royalties from an Elvis hit topped royalties from the majority of other singers.)

Once, a film producer asked Parker what he thought of a script for Elvis. The Colonel quipped, "That'll be $25,000 extra."

Parker's longtime joke: His autobiography was to be called, "How Much Does it Cost if it's Free?" and advertisements in the book sold for $25,000.

HOW MUCH DOES IT COST IF IT'S FREE?

While Parker claimed everything he was doing was for "his boy," some things definitely were not. Elvis had a huge international following. The Official Elvis Fan Club is in England, yet Elvis never toured the lucrative markets outside the US. Why not? Albert Goldman uncovered the hottest Parker hoax of all. Parker was not born in West Virginia at all, but in the town of Breda, in the southern part of the Netherlands. The long lost son of Adam van Kuijk, he was born Andreas Cornelis van Kuijk, and nicknamed "Dries." In 1929, at age 18, Dries came to America and never left the country again. Elvis never toured abroad because Parker lacked a passport.

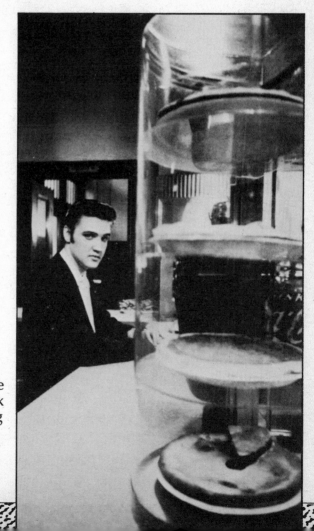

In 1957, when Elvis was earning millions, Scotty Moore and Bill Black were earning $150 a week ($250 on the road). They quit.

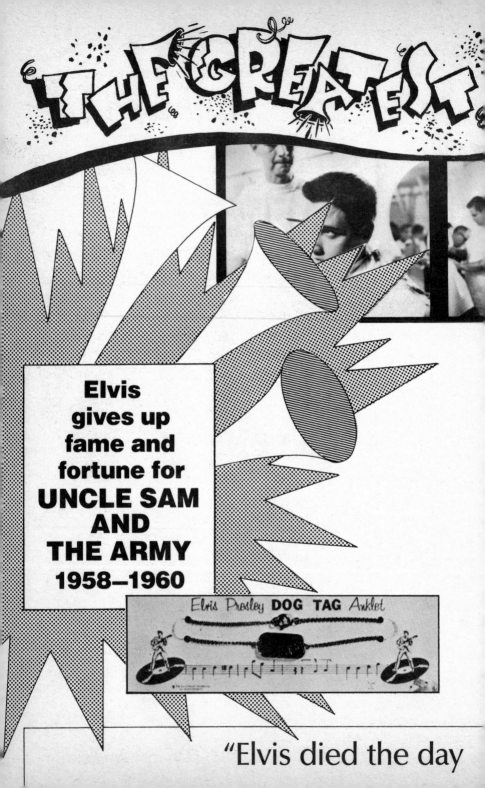

THE GREATEST

Elvis gives up fame and fortune for UNCLE SAM AND THE ARMY 1958–1960

Elvis Presley DOG TAG Anklet

"Elvis died the day

BOY ON EARTH

Parker's plan to make Elvis serve in the army was like God's plan—mysterious, and not necessarily for the best. Some theories:

—Elvis's career was at a low point after the Army; Elvis would be completely dependent on Parker to revive it.

—It gave the Colonel a chance to reshape Elvis's image.

—It gave the Colonel a challenge. "I consider it my patriotic duty to keep Elvis in the 50% tax bracket."

he went into the Army."– John Lennon

FALL OF ROCK:

JERRY
LEE
LEWIS

BLACKLISTED
FOR MARRYING HIS
14 YEAR OLD COUSIN;
HE WAS ALREADY MARRIED

CHUCK
BERRY

ARRESTED
FOR CONSPIRING
TO HAVE SEX
WITH A 14 YEAR OLD

Five months into boot camp in Killeen, Texas, Elvis faced the most critical emotional experience of a mama boy's life—mama's death. Gladys was his rock of Gibraltar, and his Juliet. Without this grounding, he fell prey to his dependencies; over the years, he became the sum of his weaknesses, not his strengths.

Gladys hadn't been healthy—she drank too much, ate poorly and overdid the diet pills, intended to combat an obesity she found embarrassing for the mother of a sex symbol. She died August 14, 1958, at age 46, probably of a heart attack spurred by acute hepatitis.

Mother's day is a key day for Elvis fans.

Enter the other woman, Priscilla Beaulieu, 14, daughter of Air Force Major Joseph Beaulieu. Enter Elvis as Humbert Humbert. (Elvis wasn't the replica of the protagonist in Nabokov's *Lolita*. Humbert was older.)

Elvis was love-struck. While both were stationed in Germany (Priscilla with her father in Wiesbaden), they dated four times a week. After Elvis moved back to Graceland in 1960, Priscilla, then 16, joined him there in 1962. Oh, Elvis, you clever cad. Not only did he convinced her father that he would "raise her respectably." He also convinced the nuns at Immaculate Conception Cathedral High School to accept, however reluctantly, his heavily mascaraed, precocious princess as a senior.

Before Elvis had recorded one note, one million orders had been placed for his new record; his 1960 return from the army was anticipated like Moses' return from the mount. As it was for Moses, reaction was not 100% positive. Teens were crushed when they realized the rebel incarnate was a would-be crooner.

Naturally, Colonel Parker had been tinkering—his point was that rebellion is just a growing-up stage. And where's a better place to symbolize reconciliation than on a stage?

For his first concert, the Colonel paired Elvis with Frank Sinatra, bobby sox idol of generations past, in Miami Beach.

TONIGHT 9:30-10:30 CH 5-33-49

ELVIS PRESLEY RETURNS TO TV

AS SPECIAL GUEST STAR ON THE
FRANK SINATRA-TIMEX SHOW
PLUS
SAMMY DAVIS, JR. · JOEY BISHOP · NANCY SINATRA

More People Buy
TIMEX Than Any Other Watch in the World

Elvis's passion was to segue from rock to movie star, but the Colonel's creation—the domesticated family pet of 1960's "G.I. Blues"—humiliated him. He dreamed of emerging as the next Brando or James Dean, but instead he became very lightweight entertainment.

Both **Flaming Star** (1960) and **Wild in the Country** (1960), the type of serious drama that Elvis hankered after, were critical and financial flops. Over the next eight years, until his 1968 Comeback Special, Elvis made 23 stock films. They became jokes—repetitious throwaways. **Kissin' Cousins**, for example, was shot in 17 days with no time for even one musical rehearsal. But they made money—by 1965, 17 films had grossed between $125–$135 million.

Was Colonel Parker Machiavellian?

UNCLE SAM

He is the wizard in **The Wizard of Oz**. He is Frank Morgan, the guy behind the big black velour with lots of gadgets and neon signs lighting up and all, and he's putting on the whole world."
—Steve Binder, producer of Elvis's Comeback Special

By the mid-sixties, wheeler-dealer Parker had made Presley the highest paid actor in Hollywood, a man who was receiving over $1 million per film plus 50% of the profits. The one problem was that he destroyed Elvis's personality and atrophied his talent in the process. More than greed, Parker's actions display a sadistic enjoyment of wielding power. Elvis despised the films, which reduced him to a laughingstock, and yet Parker continued to obligate him with long-term contracts. Elvis despised recording the schlocky soundtracks, and yet by 1964 that's all he was allowed to record.

WHY DID ELVIS ALLOW BECOME THE

1 DEPENDENT PERSONALITY

Remember his reliance on his mother ("When she yelled at me, I thought she hated me, but now I know she was only doing it for my own good")?

2 WEAKENING EGO

Removed from live performance, he lacked the hysterical mass approval which inspired and allowed braggadocio.

Chronic, sarcastic movie reviews made him feel like fluff adrift in Hollywood, a town he considered full of intellectuals.

3 THE QUICKSAND EFFECT

The more frustrated he was, the more depressed and apathetic he became, the more he needed someone to tell him what to do. Since he knew nothing about business, and desperately needed a career, he clung more and more to Parker.

THE COLONEL SAYS "HA

HIMSELF TO COLONEL'S PUPPET?

Elvis had shown lack of discrimination and laziness before. If he had had more guts, he could have told Parker where to put his "latest travelogue." But he didn't, and the Colonel knew where to hit him. A combination of Parker's strengths and Elvis's weaknesses are to blame.

The Boy in the Bubble

"It was like when you're stoned and nothing changes. They could be dropping atom bombs and you're inside Elvis's life and it doesn't matter. It just goes on and on."

"He created his own world. He had to. There was nothing else for him to do."

—Elvis acquaintances

Patients with a condition called *severe combined immuno-deficiency* cannot stand exposure to the outer world, and seem to age rapidly. You could make the same case, metaphorically, for Elvis. When he died, a hospital employee said, "He had the arteries of an 80-year-old man. His body was just worn out."

The Memphis Mafia

Is it Elvis's fault that he wanted to create a perfect world? Only that the urge proved fatal. In his gloom, Elvis surrounded himself with the Memphis Mafia, who responded like geiger counters to Elvis's every tremor, seizure or mood swing.

Men like Sonny and Red West, and Marty Lacker dated back to high school days. Others in the Mafia inner circle were Alan Fortas, Joe Esposito, Lamar Fike and Charlie Hodge. They sheltered Elvis completely from the outside world. Their inner world had its own rhythms, rituals, even language, and became more bizarre and exaggerated in the 70s.

COME OUT FROM UNDER THE COVERS, ELVIS— THERE'S NOTHING WRONG WITH YOUR HAIR

Look out! It's a FLYING TELEVISION!

That's a **beaut** of a Caddy, Elve . . .

Go on, then, it's yours. And take a grand for gas.

Elvis's "usual" was burnt bacon, mashed potatoes, corn bread in butter milk and peanut butter and jelly sandwiches

Every night was party night at Elvis's Bel Air mansion. A hot horde of girls would hang out, drinking Cokes and watching TV, idling with the guys but hoping the boss would choose to muscle his way in.

Elvis was so isolated he had no idea of the price of a can of soda.

Elvis, don't shoot Robert Goulet again . . .

BLAA

No . . . no . . . I'm **TOO FAT!**

Lamar to kitchen . . . come in, kitchen. Better get in ten cases of yogurt. It's gonna be one of those days. Over and out.

He was totally nocturnal. Once, when he was in the hospital, he had the staff put aluminum foil on the windows and reverse their entire schedules.

One house had a changing room for girls who were going swimming. Surprise, surprise! What they thought was a mirror was actually a window for the guys to peep through.

Elvis buys a Cadillac covered with 40 coats of paint containing crushed diamonds and oriental fish scales. Filled inside with gold-covered gadgets, the ceiling plated with gold records, it's an American version of Versailles.

Elvis reads his favorite book, The Physicians Desk Reference, full of information about drugs, a sign of what's to come . . .

AAM!

Oh, well, another TV blown.

Elvis's retreat was ironic. The world was his oyster—he opened it, got inside and closed the shell. The 60s art that was about to explode was kinetic, pop, raw, sex-based, black-inspired and value-smashing—as was Elvis's art. You could say he was the father of the 60s. And yet, when the Beatles visited him in his Bel Air home in 1964, they had nothing to say.

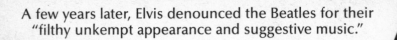

A few years later, Elvis denounced the Beatles for their
"filthy unkempt appearance and suggestive music."

The Fab Four

THE SIXTIES

New twist in Café Society Adults now dig Juves' New Beat
—Variety headline

The Freewheelin' Bob Dylan

"Bangs   manes   bouffants   beehives   Beatle caps   butter faces
brush-on lashes   decal eyes   puffy sweaters   French thrust bras
flailing leather   blue jeans   stretch pants   stretch jeans
honey-dew bottoms   eclair shanks   elf boots   ballerinas   knight slippers,
hundreds of them, these flaming little buds, bobbing and screaming,
rocketing around inside the Academy of Music Theater underneath that
vast old mouldering cherub dome up there——aren't they super-
marvelous!"   —Tom Wolfe

Before 1960, pop culture had the status of a calling card printed on a paper bag. But suddenly, anything smacking of hoi polloi was hip. What happened? The avant-garde (and the rich and hip behind them) deemed their struggle against the "spiritual wasteland," i.e. mass culture,

backward. The artists used mass culture to make statements . . . the others dove like condemned sinners into the pleasures of Hell. Everyone who was anyone was twisting at the Peppermint Lounge. It was simply radical chic, and a watershed period of contemporary culture.

1960

FDA approves first public sale of birth control pills

1961

President Kennedy sends first combat-level troops to South Vietnam

Cuban Missile Crisis

Supreme Court bans prayer in public schools

1962

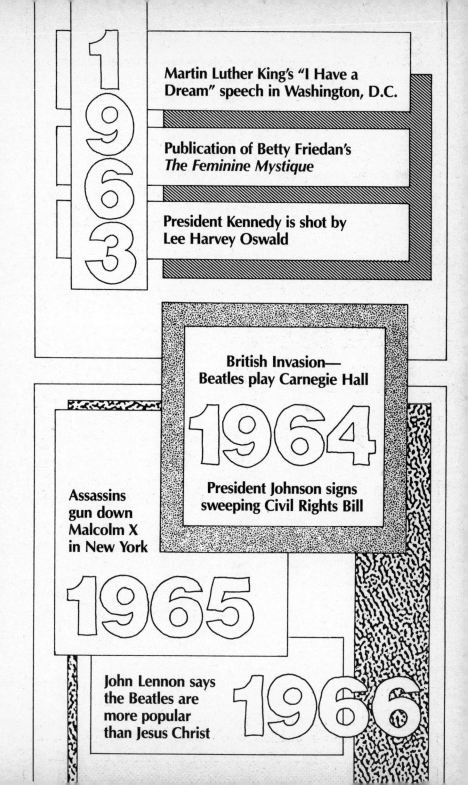

1963

Martin Luther King's "I Have a Dream" speech in Washington, D.C.

Publication of Betty Friedan's *The Feminine Mystique*

President Kennedy is shot by Lee Harvey Oswald

British Invasion— Beatles play Carnegie Hall

1964

President Johnson signs sweeping Civil Rights Bill

Assassins gun down Malcolm X in New York

1965

John Lennon says the Beatles are more popular than Jesus Christ

1966

Here's what's happening, baby, ooh mammy-o. Rock became an industry, big, we're talking big. You know, Phil Spector, a runt, he was a millionaire at 21, he was the youngest record-label chief in history, he was a genius, took pop into the hands of the young, created the Crystals, the Ronettes, lay it down, that wall of Spector sound, gotta have a sound, babydoll, like that other cat, Berry Gordy, he was happening! He had a sound, the Motown sound, started from nothing and he made the Supremes, the Temptations, the Miracles, had Mary Wells, Gladys Knight, Little Stevie Wonder, by 1964 he was selling 12 million records a year!

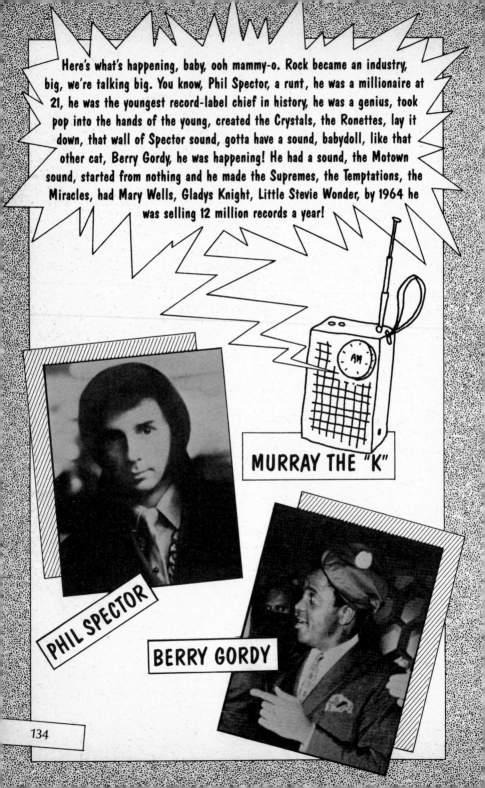

MURRAY THE "K"

PHIL SPECTOR

BERRY GORDY

In 1964, when the Rolling Stones were singing "19th Nervous Breakdown," Elvis was singing "Viva Las Vegas." While Elvis was really square, in two ways he was ultra hip, so hip he could have been Andy Warhol's biggest idol. Listen to Warhol explain how he got the idea for his series of money paintings:

"It was on one of those evenings when I'd asked around ten or fifteen people for suggestions that finally one lady friend of mine asked me the right question: 'Well, what do you love most?' That's how I started painting money."

Warhol was presenting a philosophy of boredom, ennui and lack of commitment. Who was living it more fully than Elvis? Both were into experimental debauchery, provoking and observing scenes . . . the difference was that Warhol was celebrating the emptiness of decadence and celebrity as a public image, whereas the embarrassed Elvis was debauching in private.

"Why argue with his kind of success? It's like telling Maxwell House to change their coffee formula when the stuff is selling like tomorrow!"—Col. Parker

SUPER FAN

1. In sum,
an Elvis fan.
As loyal, fanatic
and indulgent as
the Mafia and they don't get paid for it. A relationship
between fan and star unequaled in any other of the arts, or
with any other rock star. However, in deflecting cause and
effect (no matter how shoddy, they applaud, adore and
buy), Elvis had no realistic feedback or incentive. An
Elvis fan may:

A. Make his or her house into a shrine.

B. Wrap pieces of lint reverently in handkerchief and
   deposit in handbag, as one woman did before the
   cameras on Elvis's Comeback Special.

C. Lobby for Congress to declare Elvis's birthday a
   national day of recognition (as did Donna Lee Crayle).

D. Glue together the pages of
   Elvis: What Happened, (a tell-
   all exposé by bodyguards Red
   West, Sonny West and David
   Hebler) whenever sighted in
   a bookstore, variety store or
   supermarket.

E. Join one of the thousands of
   fan clubs all over the world
   (i.e., Elvis Crusaders, Blue
   Hawaiians for Elvis, The Never
   Ending Elvis Fan Club of
   Ireland, The Elvis Presley Fan
   Club of Norway, Today
   Tomorrow and Forever
   Fan Club).

On May 1, 1967, after living together for five years, Elvis marries Priscilla in a ceremony of 14 people at Las Vegas's Aladdin Hotel.

"She looked like she had about eight people living in her hair."
—Marty Lacker

Fans send hundreds of pink booties, dolls, blankets and dresses. Elvis spoils her. Seven years later, he named his private airplane The Lisa Marie to impress her.

Did he want to? Once, when asked if he'd marry, Elvis quipped, "Why buy a cow when you can get free milk?"

Elvis both spoils and isolates her.

Exactly nine months later, on February 1, 1968, Priscilla gives birth to Lisa Marie.

"I'm a happy, but shaky man."—Elvis

In 1968, a decade after his last big, big year, Elvis makes the NBC-Singer Special, a combination of slick skits and rough, intimate concert footage produced by Steve Binder. It was a smash. The adjectives used to describe him—devastating, killer, animal—make you wonder what women want.

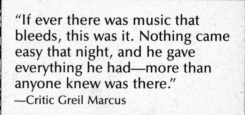

"If ever there was music that bleeds, this was it. Nothing came easy that night, and he gave everything he had—more than anyone knew was there."
—Critic Greil Marcus

"Onstage I make love to 25,000 people, then I go home alone."
—Janis Joplin

"In this world there are only two tragedies. One is not getting what one wants, and the other is getting it."
—Oscar Wilde

After the spectacular comeback, the Colonel put his boy back on the road starting in Las Vegas. It was received as a supernatural resurrection, and Elvis played it up. In his white jeweled Sun King jumpsuit, he was untouchable icon, Christ and Superman. He took his musical theme from the nationalistic Strauss ("Also Sprach Zarathustra", the 2001 Theme). He symbolized the American volk with his "American trilogy"—a medley of "Dixie," "Battle Hymn of the Republic" and a black spiritual "All My Trials." The "drop in the pit" is the true measure of Vegas success, rather than the take at the door. When Elvis played, slot machine revenues doubled. For the first time, ladies rooms stocked underwear for women who lost it when Elvis appeared.

Shopping List, 1975

$18,000	ring to Vegas guard
$10,000	Mark IV for girlfriend Melissa
$10,000	Car for girlfriend Cathy Jo
$150,000	14 Cadillacs, including $11,500 El Dorado to passing stranger
$1,750,000	Lisa Marie jet (plus three other multiengined planes)
	treatment for dog Getlo at kidney dialysis unit, Baptist hospital in Boston plus suite in the Copley Plaza Hotel
$55,000	ring for Elvis, 11½ carat diamond
$50,400	alimony to Priscilla
$48,000	Lisa Marie
	(in 1976 came $16,000 for 22 massive peanut butter-and-jelly sandwiches; includes transportation from Memphis-Denver-Memphis)

Elvis spends the rest of his life a slave to thousands of concerts. Boredom and meglomania grow side by side. Sinking deeper into fantasy, Elvis actually sinks into debt. He fancies himself a redeemer (provides extravagant gifts for strangers, studies spiritualism with a guru), a healer (pays hospital bills for strangers, lays on hands and dispenses pills) and an enforcer (owns an arsenal of guns, studies karate). Indicative of his erratic behavior, his weight swings wildly (between 190–250).

"The king is always killed by his courtiers. He is overfed, overindulged, overdrunk to keep him tied to his throne. Most people in the position never wake up."
—John Lennon on what killed Presley

"They mothered him to death."
—Dr. George Nichopoulous

To be fair to Elvis, massive fame—the distortion of every relation with the world—is a natural tie-in to insanity. Everyone belongs to you, bodily, but no part of your being is your own. Dr. Nick's comment is ironic because it was none other than he who "mothered" Elvis with drug prescriptions requiring eight full-sized legal pads to list. Everyone needs a good shot in the arm, but really. . .

PARTY VEGETABLE

Elvis was as much a drug fiend as a Janis Joplin or a Jimi Hendrix, whose legacies rest on the sex/drugs/rock 'n roll credo. Two things separated Presley from the drugs as liberation orgy of the 60s. One, that he took prescription drugs conveys a different attitude—less bohemian than embarrassed. His actions and philosophy conflicted like homosexuals who enter the priesthood. Two, as a result he kept his image as clean as Pat Boone's (by demanding total muteness from his staff). He never tried to reform and *become* Boone—instead, he turned his guilt into rage that he directed at himself and others.

(Naturally, fans refused to believe this. They claim that Elvis took drugs only to ease the pain of a colon problem.)

In 1973, Elvis divorced Priscilla after she left him for another man, karate teacher Mike Stone. A serious blow to the Elvis ego.

In 1970, Elvis offered his fervent aid to President Nixon's fight against Americans No. 1 problem—drugs. Nixon gave Elvis a Bureau of Narcotics and Dangerous Drugs badge. Elvis gave Nixon a Colt .45.

The President and the King

DEATH

"Elvis Has Left
the Building"
—J.D. Sumner (One
of the many Elvis
tribute songs
recorded at the
time of his death)

FTD's biggest day in history: The national floral network took some 2,155 orders for arrangements. Every bud in Memphis was bought. Flowers came in the guise of Bibles, crosses, crowns and guitars.

Elvis was a product of a pre-political era: his funeral proved to be the biggest and most surprising unifying national event since the generation gap began. Even in death his magnetism was stunning. Caroline Kennedy compared the Graceland scene of 30,000 mourners to India, and in many ways it was—in the gross, unrelieved suffering, human sacrifice (women broke their marriages, spent their savings, brought their babies to be there), random cruelties of fate (two girls were killed by a hit-and-run driver) and sick vulture-hustling (someone was selling sheets from the ambulance stretcher).

DAILY ☉ NEWS

FINAL

ELVIS PRESLEY DIES AT 42

Singer Suffers Heart Attack

Berkowitz Pleads Innocent; Plans Insanity Defense

Elvis Presley, one of the pioneers of rock and roll, dies in Memphis.
Stories on page 3; other pictures in the centerfold

Elvis: Idol of Millions—

NEW YORK POST METRO

MILLIONS MOURN PRESLEY

EXCLUSIVE *New book tells of his decline in a drug nightmare*

It was a standing joke among musicians not to release a record during this time. Not only were RCA's pressing plants going 24 hours a day, but they'd subcontracted every pressing plant in the country to supply the demand for Elvis records.

When he heard Elvis had died, Colonel Parker said, "Nothing has changed. This won't change anything."

Presley made more money in his first post-mortem year than he had in any year alive.

The National Enquirer sold 6.7 million copies, its all-time record, of an issue whose cover photo showed Elvis in his casket.

Elvis's death was originally listed as cardiac arrhythmia; a scandal ensued when it was uncovered as drug-related (and the hospital was in on the cover-up).

Dr. Nick was eventually acquitted on 14 counts of "willingly and feloniously" overprescribing Presley drugs, including over 19,000 doses in the last 31½ months of his life.

A Memphis judge handling the estate proceedings became appalled at improprieties of Colonel Parker's management: deals in which he made more than his client, bookings at the International Hotel in Las Vegas where he tallied over $1 million in gambling losses annually (conflict of interest), his 50% commission even after his client's death. At the court's order, the Presley estate sued. In 1982, Parker relinquished his control over by selling all his Elvis interests to RCA for $2 million. He's now writing a book about Elvis.

Lisa Marie is the sole heir to the estate estimated at $10 million and growing as royalties accumulate. She inherits it in 1993, when she turns 25.

Chief executor of the estate, Priscilla, has been a boutique owner, model and TV actress. She recently published a book, *Elvis and Me*. Rumor has it that she wanted to write a loving memoir, but her publishing company, Putnam, insisted on a little dirt.

Vernon died on May 26, 1979 in Memphis of heart failure.

> "I guess you could say Elvis was what we'd like to be. He's one of us— and yet he's our ideal."
> —a fan

The record industry Elvis left behind in 1977, now earning $3½ billion in record and tape sales, was bursting the seams of its leisure suit. It was a mainstream industry that left experimentation to science. It financed proven superstars (in '79, Paul Simon signed a $14 million contract with Warner Brothers for seven albums) and highly sophisticated studio techniques (in '79 Fleetwood Mac's *Tusk* album cost $1 million to record). Just as "Blue Suede Shoes" was piped into elevators as Muzak, the raw sting of early rock 'n roll was long gone.

ELVIS' LAST INTERVIEW

EXCLUSIVE

THE DAY HE SAID GOODBYE

BY EU

I N
wi
as
ter, w
that
give
ing
acce
joke
and
sist

zi
P
de
b

FACT!

Vital evidence concerning the cause of Elvis' death has either

suppressed or

THE KING IS GONE.

After the June tour ended, Elvis returned to Memphis. The next tour wasn't due to get underway until mid-August, giving him longer than usual to rest up. He visited Tupelo in July, staying with old family friends. Lisa flew into Memphis as soon as school was out, to spend part of her summer vacation with her daddy. In the early morning hours of 16th August, Elvis rented Libertyland, a theme park built on the site of the old Memphis Fairgrounds that he had rented privately so often in the past. For several hours, he enjoyed watching Lisa and her friends trying out the rides and attractions; the Zippin Pippin roller coaster and the Fender Bender

"Ginger called out to him, but there was no reply . . ."

Soon after, unable to sleep, Elvis took up a religious book and went into his luxurious bathroom to read. Ginger fell asleep, awakening hours later to find that Elvis wasn't there. Ginger called out to him, but there was no reply . . .

In the U.S.A., Elvis' latest disc, "Way down," stood at No. 1 on the Country Music charts. Thousands of fans held tickets for a 12-day tour due to commence in Maine on 17th August, and wind up in Memphis on 28th August. In Britain, 2000 fans were looking forward to the 21st Anniversary Annual Fan Club Convention being staged in Nottingham during the coming weekend.

When the unexpected radio and TV news flashes echoed around the world, they set off shock waves of gigantic, unprecedented proportion. Elvis, dead of a heart attack? It wasn't true, it couldn't be true. Not Elvis,

Punk was an attack on this baroque period of rock, aiming to strip back to the classic, hungry raunch of Elvis and rockabilly. It may seem funny that Elvis's mythic reputation—as rock's touchstone, ground zero, its remedy for all ills—comes from the first two years of a 23-year career. But Elvis 54–56 was like a peak experience—moments which are preserved and isolated as reference points of one's ideal.

FACT!
The tragic events leading up to Elvis' last day on earth have only recently been revealed.

PRISCILLA AND LISA MARIE TODAY

How Elvis' Only Wife And Daughter Are Facing The Future...

Lisa M...
veillance
beginnin...
curiosity
her da...
harm. ...
might ...
Presle...
To...
a Bev...
ed e...
Mar...
with ...
att...
A...
b...
c...

This is what happened to Elvis in the last 24-hours he was alive. At 11 PM on August 15, 1977. Elvis left Graceland with Ginger Alden and went to an appointment with his dentist, Lester Hoffman. At 1:30 AM on August 16, they returned to the Memphis mansion and Elvis went to his room where he turned on the TV set. Elvis was starting on a national concert tour that very day and he was trying to relax. At 4 AM. Elvis decided to play raquetball so he called his cousin Billy Smith and his wife Jill. At 4:30, Elvis, Ginger, Billy and Jill left to play at the raquetball court. After a while, Elvis stopped playing ball and started playing the piano. They were back

"MY CHERISHED MEMORIES OF ELVIS"

REMEMBER ELVIS

n,
lim Best

"**A** whole industry was built around an animated mouse named Mickey. The next could be Elvis Presley."
—Joseph Rascoff, Presley estate business manager

"**W**e are trying hard to actually give birth to him again."
—Joseph Rascoff

Gold & platinum Elvis doll	$275
Porcelain Elvis doll	$2,500
Love Me Tender Candy Bar	$75
Original **Speedway** Album	$1,200
Aloha from Hawaii (with special "Chicken of the Sea" sneak preview sticker on cover)	$1,000
Moody Blue single on colored vinyl	$1,000
TV Guide presents Elvis Presley	$1,000

Posthumously Presley—the biggest money-maker of all. Elvis may have died, but he's still making money hand over fist—Presleyana is close to billion dollar business. Opened as a museum in 1982, Graceland annually grosses nearly $7 million (535,000 visitors spend an average of $12.80). A 1984 Tennessee law ruled that the Presley estate has unqualified right to control all use of his name and likeness—therefore, all royalties go to the estate.

Elvis Presley, the former Herbert Baer, was the first Elvis impersonator to legally change his name.

Hundreds of impersonators exist, working in Chicago, Vegas, New York and abroad. Elvis's stepmother, Dee Presley, manages impersonator Elvis Wade. (If they married, he'd still be Elvis Wade.)

It's too bad Elvis wasn't cloned. But with the latest technology, people are doing their best to reincarnate the King. For his 50th birthday celebration, RCA made a Blue Suede Shoes video, intercutting old footage with a young, thin actor-Elvis. Soon that awkward splicing will be unnecessary. Using a process called computer compositing, computer scientists will be able to recreate the image of a dead person onscreen—talking, moving, speaking. Aloha, Elvis!

No one rock star has galvanized attention the way Elvis did. The Beatles did it with four; Michael Jackson came close (perhaps merged with Prince the two would make an Elvis); the Live Aid concert came closest to the kind of world synchronicity Elvis offered. But at a time when it was younger and more innocent, America took Elvis as its first love, and there is only one first love. He was a rebel when there was room to shock. The major shock now is future shock. Stars face quick turnover and an easy slide into obsolescence, driven by the public's cranky boredom and cravings for something new.

The black megastar has finally come into its own (include Prince, Jackson, Lionel Richie); so has the female (Madonna, Cyndi Lauper, Tina Turner). Pop music now draws without a moment's notice from any new development in black music. In 1984, the dance-rhythm charts dictated the pop hits. Rapping and breakdancing went straight from the ghetto to the suburbs as the year's fads. This so-called "hip hop" culture took music back to the essentials of African music—voice, beat and spontaneity—while experimenting with the major innovations in recent pop music—electronics and computers.

The introduction and general acceptance of video clips to accompany records united America's two favorite art forms; music and film. It also widened the possibility for innovation, i.e. mixed media performances of the avant-garde. MTV, the cable video network, became a phenomenal commercial success, spawning numerous imitators. Because of its massive national audience, MTV became a maker and breaker of hits, a power broker of unprecedented proportion.

The consolidation of record companies left a handful of dominant conglomerations and little room for smaller adventurers. Most music is too much under the corporate thumb, but good music leaks out. The popularity of rock is still growing, a testament to the strange, but virile life and times of rock 'n roll.

"We are all in the gutter,
but some of us are looking at the stars."
—Oscar Wilde

ELVIS TESTIMONIALS

Bing Crosby "The things that he did during his career, the things he created are something really important."

Bono, lead singer of U2 "Elvis could say more in somebody else's song than Albert Goldman could say in any book!"

Bruce Springsteen "There have been a lotta tough guys. There have been pretenders. There have been contenders. But there is only one king . . . Everything starts and ends with him. He wrote the book."

Ian Hunter "Elvis had animal magnetism. He was even sexy to guys. I can't imagine what chicks used to think."

Eddie Murphy "Elvis was the greatest entertainer who ever lived."

George C. Wallace "Elvis was one of the greatest entertainers of all time."

Peter Frampton "Elvis was one of the greatest entertainers and one of the most influential forces of the century."

Jimmy Carter (official White House release) "Elvis Presley's death deprives us our country of a part of itself. He was unique; and irreplaceable . . . His following was immense and he was a symbol to people the world over, of the vitality, rebelliousness, and good humor of his country."

Albert Goldman "One of the greatest problems was trying to find something positive to say about this man."

Steve Allen "The fact that someone with so little ability became the most popular singer in history says something significant about our cultural standards."

Abbie Hoffman "He wasn't a real sinner, and he sure as hell wasn't a saint. Elvis didn't die for our sins, he left us here to do it on our own."

Zurich headline "Vier Dinge hat Amerika der Welt gegeben" (four things has American given the world) Baseball, Mickey Mouse, Coca-Cola und Elvis."

BIBLIOGRAPHY

Elvis

Dundy, Elaine. **Elvis and Gladys**. New York: MacMillan, 1985.

Dunleavy, Steve with Red West, Sonny West and Dave Hebler, **Elvis: What Happened?** New York: Ballantine, 1977.

Goldman, Albert. **Elvis.** New York: MacGraw-Hill Books, 1981.

Gregory, Neal and Janice. **When Elvis Died.** Washington, D.C.: Communications Press, 1980.

Hopkins, Jerry. **Elvis.** New York: Simon and Schuster, 1971.

Hopkins, Jerry. **The Final Years.** New York: St. Martin's Press, 1980.

Farren, Mick and Marchbank, Pearce. **Elvis in his Own Words**. New York: Omnibus Press, 1977.

Mann, May. **Elvis and the Colonel.** New York: Pocket Books, 1976.

Presley, Priscilla. **Elvis and Me.** New York: Putnam Publishing Group, 1985.

Tharpe, Jac, ed. **Elvis: Images and Fancies.** Jackson, Miss.: University Press of Mississippi, 1979.

Torgoff, Martin, ed. **The Complete Elvis.** New York: Delilah Communications, 1982.

Worth, Fred L. and Tamerius, Steve K. **All About Elvis.** New York: Bantam Books, 1981.

Wertheimer, Albert. **Elvis '56: In the Beginning.** New York: Collier, 1979.

Rock History and Sociology

Cohn, Nik. **Rock from the Beginning.** New York: Stein and Day, 1969.

Escott, Colin and Hawkins, Martin. **Catalyst: The Sun Records Story.** London: Aquarius Books, 1975.

Frith, Simon. **Sound Effects.** New York: Pantheon Books, 1981.

Gillett, Charlie. **The Sound of the City.** New York: Pantheon Books, 1970, 1983.

Guralnick, Peter. **Lost Highway.** New York: Vintage Books, 1979.

Hibbard, Don and Kaleialoha, Carol. **The Role of Rock.** Englewood Cliffs, NJ: Prentice-Hall, Inc., 1983.

Laing, Dave. **The Sound of Our Time.** Chicago: Quadrangle Books, 1969.

Marcus, Greil. **Mystery Train.** New York: E.P. Dutton, 1976.

Marsh, Dave and Stein, Kevin. **The Book of Rock Lists.** New York: Dell Publishing, 1981.

Miller, Jim, ed. **The Rolling Stone Illustrated History of Rock & Roll.** Rolling Stone Press/Random House, 1976.

Tosches, Nick. **Unsung Heroes of Rock 'n' Roll.** New York: Charles Scribner's Sons, 1984.

Tosches, Nick. **Hellfire.** New York: Dell Publishing, 1982.

Blues

Bane, Michael. **White Boy Singin' the Blues.** New York: Penguin Books, 1982.

Baraka, Imamu Amiri (Jones, Leroi). **Blues People.** New York: William Morrow, 1963.

Guralnick, Peter. **Feel like Going Home.** New York: Outerbridge & Dienstfrey, 1971.

Hirshey, Gerri. **Nowhere to Run: The Story of Soul Music.** New York: Times Books, 1984.

Keil, Charles. **Urban Blues.** Chicago: University of Chicago Press, 1956.

McKee, Margaret and Chisenhall, Fred. **Beale Black & Blue.** Baton Rouge: Louisiana State University Press, 1981.

Murray, Albert. **Stompin' the Blues.** New York: MacGraw-Hill, 1976.

Palmer, Robert. **Deep Blues.** New York: The Viking Press, 1981.

Country Music

Green, Douglas. **Country Roots.** New York: Hawthorn Books, 1976.

Grissim, John. **Country Music: White Man's Blues.** New York: Paperback Library, 1970.

Hemphill, Paul. **The Nashville Sound: Bright Lights and Country Music.** New York: Simon and Schuster, 1970.

Kochman, Marilyn, ed. **The Big Book of Bluegrass.**
New York: Quill/Frets Books, 1984.
Malone, Bill. **Country Music U.S.A.: A fifty year history.**
Austin: University of Texas Press, 1968.
Morthland, John. **The Best of Country Music.** Garden City,
NY: Doubleday & Co., 1984.
Tosches, Nick. **Country.** New York: Stein and Day, 1977.

Social History/Pop culture

Cleaver, Eldridge. **Soul on Ice.** New York: Dell Publishing,
1968.
Dickstein, Morris. **Gates of Eden.** New York:
Basic Books, 1977.
Lewis, George, ed. **Side-Saddle on the Golden Calf.** Pacific
Palisades, Calif.: Goodyear Publishing Co., 1972.
Obst, Lynda. **The Sixties.** New York: Rolling Stone Press/
Random House, 1977.
Warhol, Andy. **Popism: The Warhol 60s.** New York:
Harper & Row, 1980.
Wolfe, Tom. **The Kandy-Kolored Tangerine-Flake Streamline
Baby.** New York: Farrar, Straus & Giroux, 1965.

Special thanks to: Marguerite Renz, RCA Records;
New York Public Library Picture Collection;
Jack Soden, Executive Director, Graceland;
Lincoln Center Sound Archives; Ann Shields